hai

The Illustrated Fox

With a chime of brush on jam jar
she drew the Totterdown fox afield,
stroked its snout to query Dundry's spire,
coloured the grey of Three Lamps,
showed it Chew and Blagdon water.

Its nightly mooch of Tesco's bins
splashed midnight Wraxall blue
but she left Brunel's bridge as a beacon,
a North Star to divine its flyover home,
let it dream of free range chicken.

Ben Banyard

also from Gert Macky Books
inking bitterns

'a gorgeous little book throughout,
with vivid snappy and tender poems...
joyfully illustrated... a must-have!"
Penelope Shuttle

hailing foxes
and other wild things

illustrated by Dru Marland

Bristol
Gert Macky Books
mmxv

first published in 2015 by
Gert Macky Books
4 Cotham Vale, Bristol, BS6 6HR
drusilla.marland@btopenworld.com
gertmacky.co.uk

printed by minutemanbristol.com

ISBN 978-0-9926783-2-6

All rights reserved
Poems © their authors
Illustrations © Dru Marland

to Katie, Llygoden and Fitzgerald,
because wildness begins at home

Contents

Early Morning in South Bristol

On the cliff face of the morning traffic's roar,
nestling into its moments, the little things
carve out the tiny particular edges of their lives.

A blackbird chooses its branch for singing;
an apple decides to fall;
a slug gnaws faceless at a rotting marrow.

My garden is a golden brandy glass.
Swilling silence round in the sun I stand
on my kitchen step, engraving the day.

Pat Simmons

Blackbird

The blackbird is a dark bird,
a shadow-feathered boy,

but he sings out from a golden bill
with little gaps for joy.

As lovely as the soaring lark,
but clear and true and strong,

he whistles and the world becomes
blackbird, blue sky, song.

Liz Brownlee

1

the names of rain
a blackbird's subsong
into dusk

Alan Summers

The Day We Came To Bristol

The day we came to Bristol
it rained, it poured
hammered down
giant splashes tap-danced off the pavements
as our stout removal team
whisked everything we owned into the house.

When it was done
we slept, exhausted
and woke to a clear sky
a beech tree shaking raindrops from its leaves
and blackbirds on the grass
bursting with song.

Pameli Benham

2

The Green Man

A world inside his jacket pocket

twigs so brittle they snap like bones,
autumn leaves that crumble to release
the faintest echo of a presence that might once
have been the scent of something

perfect

mint, eucalyptus, freedom

horseradish root tangled in garden twine,
coasters from The Rummer
where he and Bert and Wally met
Monday nights for a few pints
over heated arguments about brassica
neat paper parcels that open to reveal
black, grey, round, oblong, spiky
unlikely seeds with faded names
antirrhinum, helianthus, paeonia albiflora

a blunt penknife, some thrupenny bits,
a rabbit's skull, keys to unlock life

and dangling from their centre ring
a plastic head sprouting vines and branches
through its open mouth, the menace
made less ominous
where his fingers over years
have rubbed it smooth.

There's hard graft, winter gusting
through the Gorge, a battered leather wallet full of fluff,
the remains of his wartime ration book,
a pencil stub.

Next spring I'll plant the seeds,
start looking forward to flowers.

4

Shirley Wright

Elgin Fox

I remember the first time that I saw a fox,
In the middle of Redland Bristol
Late at night.
Its eyes bright beads of night-time bijouterie
Flashing in the sodium glare.
I remember the first time that I saw fox prints
Etched in the lawn's smooth, pre-dawn snow.
In recent years these visits have increased.
Daylight forays along streets and in gardens.
Sniffing the bins at the local "cop-shop".
The fox's beauty still captures my eye,
But its manner is now almost brazen.
A visiting friend delights in the sight
And we delight in revealing our Reynard,
Crossing the grass and leaping up onto
Our hand-crafted, English Oak table.
"Aaah, how sweet - How cute,
How lovely - You brute!"
That's disgusting. Revolting. It's pissing
All over the fine-grained surface of our oak table.
He's marking his claim to the territory.
My territory! Our territory! Not his!
"Piss off! Get lost!"
He leaps to the ground and runs to the shed,
Where later I tread in his droppings.
Nature is wondrous. Nature is shit.

From rarity to lavatory. From wonder to disgust.
How fickle are my feelings.
I love:
Nature on the telly; nature in the press;
Nature captured vividly by digital eyes.
But don't let it bite me, sting me or fight me.
Don't let it crap, where I might be eating.
Leave it in the pages of National Geographic.
Send Bear Grylls to wrestle with the crocs.
But keep me at a distance
From that peeing urban fox.

David C Johnson

Wilding the Urb

Not knowing wind's salt taste
harsh cry, or dive's swift chill,
wriggle of fish in his beak; only
alley restaurant bins, tourists
fisting sticky buns and church-cliff
colonies, roof gullies.

She's never padded an earth-path
by stubble-fields for rabbit, or sheep scent,
nor discovered the allure of henhouse.
Only shady garden corners
wheelie-bins, greasy chicken bones
in cardboard coats.

The narrow steeple makes a perch
for falcon, returning each year to breed,
there's enough height to dive
for pigeon fodder, rat scuttle;
safe from predators and all those eyes
gazing up with their scopes.

Rachael Clyne

A fox's late winter blessing

May soil go soft beneath your claws
to give you beetles grubs and worms
the alleyways be full of food, the roots
and stones conspire to keep you dry.

May your nose know all the languages
of dead and living. May everything
by its nose learn your range and kin,
your songs shake sleepers from their dreams.

May cats and dogs who think they're hard
see your teeth and think agin.
May seagulls never get there first,
and wires and highways not restrain you.

On long green evenings or belated dawns,
may your own kits play on and on,
moon after moon, and even after
this city itself has gone.

Dominic Fisher

Heaney's Wake

All year,
from winter to autumn, I see them
most evenings –

on high streets, down side-roads
slipping through hedges
under the bunting of parked cars,
charcoal running stitches
hemming the edge of dark. In April
vixens trail their kits
                            like knots
                                in hankies

Come September
            flashes of amber – intermittent –
a youngster, trapped by headlights
                    panics on Southmead Road
                        spins in indecision,
his current short-circuiting, every nerve and instinct
                                scrambled

After the wake
and the long drive back,
two miles from home and my bed
the shadows in my head give way to quick
anticipation

a dog-fox on Horfield Common
in Belisha beacon glare
waits for me to brake, trots over the crossing
with a twitch of his white-tipped tail. If I could
touch his fur, sparks would
jump and crackle

my spirits kindled by this sight,
this flaring matchstick
to hold against the night

Deborah Harvey

Wells Road Madness

We see a mouse in her house, bold as you like,
skitter across laminate floor, behind the whatnot.

We scrabble to the kitchen, to lunch leftovers, a bit of brie,
smoked salmon, lock'em in the fridge; reach for Yellow
Pages.

Then halfway to Broadwalk in traffic crawl, a sleek black
shape
darts through cars, streaks through a gateway

wriggle-tail as it disappears into laurel bushes –
a mink determined to escape being someone's coat.

A car pulls up, a woman starts searching. Her pet?
A mink pet? Surely not; but odd things happen in Totterdown.

Rachael Clyne

Not seeing kingfishers

The story my life is telling
cannot be found in a five year plan

neither is it written in a list
of Things To Do Before I Die.

It is like
looking for kingfishers at Siston Brook

returning again and again, watching and waiting
for that hit of blue, green, orange

knowing that somewhere in all the green overhang
at the water's edge hides a secret

and each time hoping that just for once
I am not too late.

Jinny Peberday

Down river

Sunlit seagulls fly
behind bare winter branches
where I must follow

Winter seagulls fly
behind bare, sunlit branches

Winter bares branches
and seagulls fly where I
must follow sunlight

Kathy Gee

Talking to a kingfisher about categories

Kingfisher, is it true -
are you really brown?
How solid is a learnt fact?

Is colour more than what we see?
Do we have colours,
or just see them?

Are fears real?
If a person dies and you didn't need them
are they really missed?

Are you still a migrant if you drown –
a little brown job -
nothing to get excited about?

Tom Sastry

conning

Those were the years we were sky pilots
captains of the roof
standing our watches up the bathroom ladder

Fearless we surveyed the oceans of the Somerset sky
sought signs in the stars
counted fireballs and marvels
steered by the sirens

Balloon time we were Ahab and Ishmael
facing down the whales that swam down to the surface
Lord, how they roared
plunged back into the sky's depths

The city is an atoll where the birds swim
diving round the reefs of houses
Magpies whisper bad dreams down chimney pots

All this is on the chart

Dru Marland

Filmic

The saddest evening of my life
is the one
where I walk around Bristol as a camera
drenched in the solitaries of autumn.

It still happens on playback.
The clocks have just bolted. A shocking dark
sky marbles the evening clouds.
I walk on the splash of leaves

I just want to tell a story
that matters.

On Somerset Street, a window throws light
onto the back of a slick cat;
a car's fat rich tyres
crunch through space like torn shirts.

You hear classical music
from the high Georgian windows. But you're following me,
my eye. It drops down
past the raucous welcome
of the Hillgrove Porter Stores
into the widescreen city below.

Silence. Gulls and sirens
and I'm here, waiting

wanting to tell a story
that matters.

Tom Sastry

I don't know who you are...

You: digging your way through St. Augustine's Marsh.
Mud up to your knees, water to your waist; squelching
through a squidge of brackish Bristol mud to cut the Great
Ditch. Deep as three men standing. Wide as two dozen men
touching outstretched fingers. Half a mile long from where
the River Frome turns aside at St Stephen's church down
to the harbour where the Arnolfini stands today.

Forgive me – but of the ghosts behind your spade it's you
I see most clearly: You are Richard Ayllard the Mayor.
You are King Henry III. You are the men of Brigstowe
and, sometimes, the men of Redcliffe. You are all of these
but especially, you're the man in the marsh, digging the first
narrow ditch of the river's new course from church to dock.

Next to it you dig another ditch. Alongside these, more
ditches; steadily widened and deepened until they merge
into one broad cutting. Your tools are mattock and spade
– and a leather bucket to scoop liquid mud into a creak
of wicker baskets which you, or yourself, haul up when

you can. As King, you must scare up more men, and write
from Bristol Castle commanding the pride of Redcliffe
to muck in: '...*lest the aforesaid work, which We regard
as our own, through your defection should receive delay...*'
Even so, it's eight years before you get to let the water in.

Then you're partying, drinking deep from a choice barrel.
But, as King, you picture London's new Bridge; think
Bristol's creaky timber crossing undignified for a city
which holds a secure and commodious harbour at its heart:
'*Then must we burn to the water our ancient wooden bridge
and rebuild, in stone a crossing more fitted to our dignity.*'

A nice change, you think fuzzily. To be a mason. To be dry...

John Terry

The Avon New Cut

Such arrogance, to pick a river up
and place it somewhere else. Such vision
or such blindness, to understand the moon's
sinewy tug, the great reaching out
of water across the arch of nothingness,
as merely a hindrance to uploading cargo
and the maintenance of shipping schedules.

Now the river hurries furtive down
its Cut, its long wound – ever new – razored
deep across Totterdown and Temple, Redcliffe,
Spike Island and Bedminster. Keeps to itself,
huddling shawl over head. Mutters mud
and madness as it oozes past the shame
of shattered rock and twisted bicycles.

But water cannot be wrong, can only follow
its deep imperative: to sink. The earth
forgives its wounds, snows the unnatural banks
with cherry, fetches forth the scurvy-grass and asters
to greet the alien salt, and settles in new
nakedness, patient and vulnerable,
to meet the scouring fingers of the sea.

Pat Simmons

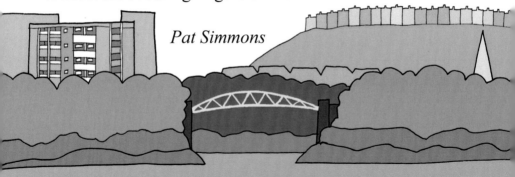

A Naturist Looks Out of Her Window in Bristol

The city sprawls, wobbling in the afternoon heat
leaf and brick competing for their share
of the bright blue horizon

Amongst the still air and dancing dust mites
the house plant squats, fat
and retired from the race

A spider cascades down the slippery green
plopping gently onto the sun-steamed carpet

She stalks the living room with brilliant finesse
like a stiletto-clad beauty
before the third prosecco

I fetch a wineglass and newspaper
scoop her, carry her, and plonk her squinting
onto the warm, glittering concrete outside

Her small brown body trudges the asphalt, in search of shade

Alas, she was a house spider, Steatoda Grossa
and I have fed her to the urban jungle

I could go outside, I could fetch her
But it is too hot

And like the plant
like the spider

Today I am a house human

Ruby Fowden-Willey

Walking to Work Whistling

after Deryn Rees-Jones

I whistled to the morning, and the sweeping concert of the
morning,
and the sun, and the shadows, and the clean light

and the trees and the kisses in the cherry tree
and I whistled the feeling of our thighs entwined, how my bed

was all in bloom, and the moonlight was in bloom
and how everything was opening now

and I whistled the robins, here and here, and here again
and I whistled the smiles, your smiles, and my smiles

and how becoming we are
how our kisses sing,

and I whistled your hair and your easy sighs,
and the shadows, and the moonlight, and there, in my bed,
with our arms around each other

and our kisses smiled,
and I whistled a happiness I haven't known till now

the cherry tree,
and the concert,
and you reading a poem to me

A compass held to the moon.
A bed bound for the stars.

Colin Brown

Cherry Blossom ll

In later years I have grown confident in springs' return
in the tender leaf, crisp tulips in others gardens

but I covet in secret the cherry tree I planted
cold makes the trunk's gloss tighten

the search for buds, when I brave the wind,
more diligent. The weak spring sunshine

loiters on stones and shoots
raindrops become precious along a leaf edge

dumb as bluebells, I stand under the cherry tree
above, the sky becomes this year's bridal lace

once the blossom comes.
I shall not always be here,

to relish my harvest
in the cold earth let the snowdrops speak for me.

Hazel Hammond

morning star
a can of cherry cola
starts to fizz

Alan Summers

20

The Shriek

High drama in Monks Park
Allie is cupping a handful of hurt
her face indignant

The crows attacked it
I heard this noise as I walked by
She uncurls her fingers, hardly dares look
One of the bastards has pecked out its eye
I didn't know that toads could shriek
Is it a toad?

I point out its motorcycle leathers
its jackhammer legs

But the frog just sits
It's hopping nowhere
Frozen. Torpid as a clod
so we settle it underneath the hedge
in a hospice of moss and sodden leaves
to take its chances

hidden from crows, those malcontents
carping and rearranging their feathers.

Deborah Harvey

Home

A peregrine grips the cliff edge nest site,
stares into the Avon-cut chasm and waits.

A pigeon fails
to fly home.

Stewart Carswell

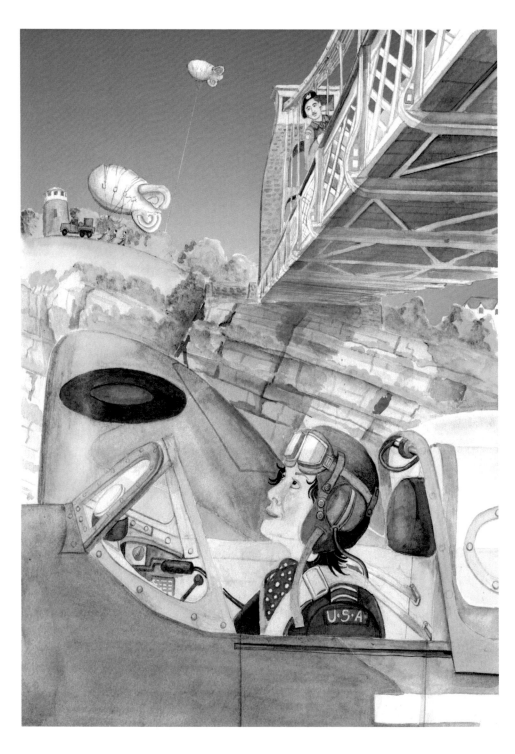

Ann Wood-Kelly flies under the Clifton Suspension Bridge

This bridge traverses so much sky,
Such sheer depth of open air
As tempts my aircraft under there;
It seemed ungrateful not to try.

I held my breath. A sudden flick
Of shadow on my face; my joy
Reflected in that waving boy;
The cliff face zipping by, so quick.

Now, zooming high, I see the far
Welsh mountains in the dawning glow
While Bristol's half asleep below,
And steer toward the morning star.

Dru Marland

Brunel's suspension bridge has proved irresistible to many pilots over
the years; possibly the largest aircraft to fly under there was a Canberra
jet bomber... Ann Wood-Kelly, an American volunteer with the ATA,
certainly flew a Spitfire under the Severn railway bridge at Sharpness;
and, if she didn't actually do the Clifton bridge as her Guardian obituary
claimed, she would have found it a doddle in comparison, if she had.

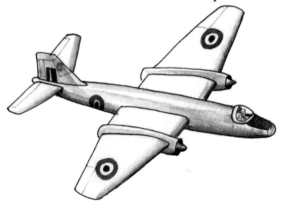

The Lunch Hour

Bristol becomes a sun-smashed corner
of the world, translucent,
holding her chin across blue skylines,
as we enter lunch time, bump elbows.

Pavements become new colours,
everyone stares their city straight in the eye
and bites down on a sandwich.

It's just a quick summer,
but we hold it with ten to two pursed lips.

Alan Summers

Painting Clouds

Between cloud bursts builders give my flat
a face lift; scars filled in, that wall greyed
with smog and dry rot is retouched to a white
that mixes with the rain and drizzles down
the walls to form puddles on the concrete floor.

While down the road the people of Stokes Croft
are painting too. The over sixties and the under
tens, students and labourers, some with homes –
others without – chat over cups of tea and
slices of cake. Old wooden doors animate

and bud beneath their fingers. Wildflowers
bloom here and deer graze on canvas in an
outcast building in Jamaica Street where there
are no flowers, only different kinds of weed,

and half-starved grey pigeons peck amongst
the refuse of the day. But in the room ships
set sail from isles of colour and cityscapes
emerge where dark storm clouds threaten.

One man's eyes seem to tell of years spent
sitting on street corners. His voice echoes
with the deepness of underpasses but his
brush transforms the canvas. He paints
the town red – and has an artists vision.

Vanessa Whiteley

Handmade

I don't come here for the organic brownies
or the fairtrade teas
I come just to sit on this chair
handmade by the hands of Tom Redfern
or so it says on the brown parcel label tied to the armrest
with garden twine

I would never get it home on the bus
all the way from Picton Street to Longwell Green
and I can't imagine paying £220 for a chair
even if it is handmade
even if it is smooth and curved in all the right places

even if it is handmade by Tom Redfern using hazel
and steam- bent beech from Barrow Woods
even though my chairs come from Ikea
and don't smell of beeswax
and I don't suppose Tom Redfern would give them a second
glance, much less run his fingers over them
searching out rough or splintered edges to hand smooth

my fingers caress the beech frame, faintly grained
handmade by Tom Redfern
his hands
his skin, softly grained

Jinny Peberday

Bewildered

It happens. One minute you're in the swim
the sea accommodates your shape
the next you turn around to find the tide gone out

and you marooned above the mud line
swamped by waves of grass
their foaming seed

That's bad enough
But imagine the water was never there
that what you thought was sea are bluebells

a thinning caul of mist. You're a boat
that didn't fall far from the tree
a ship in a forest

and this the glade where you will rot
unaccustomed to the current's tug
the taste of salt

Deborah Harvey

This poem is in part inspired by Luke Jerram's installation of fishing
boats in Leigh Woods, high above the Avon Gorge, in the spring and
summer of 2015.

28

The English and Welsh Grounds Lightship

Some ships are bound for Newport Docks,
and they pass to the west of us;
And the Sharpness and the Bristol boats sail safely to the east
And the flood tide that sometimes roars
enough to fright the best of us
Uplifts us, but it will not shift our anchorage the least.

There as always is the chimney of the Uskmouth power station,
Lined up with the Transporter Bridge and distant Ysgyryd Fawr;
And the goods trains wind away
with all the produce of the nations
While our newspapers are out of date
and week-old milk's gone sour.

Still, there's tab nabs at smokoe, after sujieing and holystone;
And a splash of conny onny that goes nicely in the tea.
And each day in the log takes me closer still to going home-
Though when I'm home I wonder if my real home's the sea.

Cos when dusk comes and we light the lamp,
and settle down to tend for it,
I look up and down the channel, and see all the lights like ours
From Flat Holm down to Countisbury;
St Brides Wentlooge; the Breaksea ship;
The beacons of the South Wales shore,
of Devon and of Somerset;
The flashing lights, the steady ones, that sparkle near and far;
One great coastal constellation, and it's we who tend the stars.

Dru Marland

The former English and Welsh Grounds light vessel now lies in Bristol's Bathurst Basin, and is used as the headquarters of the Cabot Cruising Club. Out in the Severn estuary, an automatic buoy now carries on its work.

tab nabs: snacks   *holystone*: a block of stone used for
smokoe: break   scouring wooden decks
sujieing: washing down   *conny onny*: condensed milk

30

the poets

Ben Banyard's debut pamphlet, *Communing*, will be published by Indigo Dreams in 2016. He edits *Clear Poetry*, a blog which showcases accessible work by newcomers and old hands alike: https://clearpoetry.wordpress.com

Pameli Benham is a Londoner now happily settled in Bristol. She acts, directs, teaches and writes, sings and dances, gardens and cooks, and sells her collection of poems *Plentiful As Blackberries* for WaterAid.

Colin Brown is much the same as everyone who loves to read, he was born long ago in a poetry book with dragonflies, robins, swallows, high hills, trees, rivers and people who went down deep mines. He has known bad and better things, danced with comrades and skallywags and wondered at secrets whispered around Tinker's Pond.

Liz Brownlee, Bristolian, loves this smiling city. She writes mainly about animals in over 60 anthologies and her book *Animal Magic*. Two more books are due in 2017. She is a National Poetry Day Ambassador, regularly visiting schools. Web: http://www.poetlizbrownlee.co.uk, Blog: http://www.lizbrownleepoet.com

Stewart Carswell is from the Forest of Dean. He has a PhD from Bristol University, and currently lives in Cambridge. His poems have recently been published in Brittle Star, Firewords, and Sarasvati

Rachael Clyne's collection, Singing at the Bone Tree, won Indigo Dreams' George Stevens Memorial Prize. She belongs to Wells Fountain Poets. Anthologies: *The Very Best of 52, Book of Love and Loss, Poems for a Liminal Age.* Magazines: *Poetry Space, Reach, The Interpreters House.*

Dominic Fisher From Bath/Bristol, he started writing poetry at school. After university at Aberystwyth, he taught English language for 33 years, publishing sporadically, before deciding to return to poetry properly. Family legend claims he is related to Edgar Allan Poe.

Ruby Fowden-Willey is currently working as an intern for Poetry Can after graduating from UWE in Film and Screenwriting. She finds inspiration for her poetry in Bristol, its people, and her experiences. She's hoping to do a masters in Creative Writing.

Kathy Gee works in museums and heritage. Since 2011 some fifty of her poems have been accepted by print and online magazines. Her first collection will be published in 2016.

Deborah Harvey's two poetry collections, *Communion* (2011) and *Map Reading For Beginners* (2014), are published by Indigo Dreams. Her novel, *Dart*, appeared under their Tamar Books imprint in 2013. Deborah is a trustee of Poetry Can, which supports the development of poetry across the south-west of England. She enjoys hill-walking with her border collie, Ted.

Hazel Hammond enjoys Bristol's cultural life, performs her poetry, blogs, became a (temporary) super hero and regularly opens her house to the local art trail. She is the author of *Needlepoint.*

David C Johnson is a witty prize-winning performance poet and Radio 4 playwright. He has appeared at literary festivals in the UK and N.America. His latest collection, *Earwig in the Radio* (Paralalia) , was published in May 2015.

Dru Marland is a sometime mariner and aspiring poet, when she isn't fixing bicycles and her Morris Traveller.

Jinny Peberday does not live in Bristol. After eighteen years of dwelling in and around the city she moved onto a pea-green boat with her partner and a tailless cat. Last seen drifting through Wiltshire in search of kingfishers.

Tom Sastry is a bureaucrat and occasional human. He co-hosts a monthly spoken word night Festival at the Eldon House in Bristol with Josh Ward.

Pat Simmons worked in marketing and communications for a number of overseas development charities, including Oxfam. Poetry has been her main obsession since her retirement.

Alan Summers, a Pushcart Prize nominated poet and author of forthcoming book *Writing Poetry: the haiku way* is featured on NHK World TV with *Europe meets Japan*. He regularly runs courses for With Words: www.withwords.org. uk

John Terry has been published in a fair number of magazines and has won a fair number of competitions. Fair enough.

Vanessa Whiteley loves Bristol's many faces. She enjoys writing about people and places and regards her poems as socially engaged.

Shirley Wright writes stuff. Her novel, *Time out of Mind,* is a ghost story set in Cornwall, and her poetry collection is called *The Last Green Field,* published by Indigo Dreams.

acknowledgements

Thanks to the city of Bristol for being such a good place to be; to the wildlife of Bristol, who just don't care; to the poets of Bristol, who give encouragement, support, criticism - and offer a thriving community that welcomes the lonely wordmonger.

Thanks, too, to that fine Bristol-based organisation, Poetry Can, at whose long-running monthly Can Openers events I mumbled my first tentative haiku in public; and especial thanks to Colin Brown, whose generous encouragement and advice helped steer this book through to publication; and Deborah Harvey, who found time in an already furiously busy life to help too.

And thank you to Peter and Lucie, who run Minuteman Press in Bedminster, and who are always very helpful and understanding with people who want to publish something and aren't quite sure how to go about it.

Dru Marland
Gert Macky Books